All Will Be Well

D0440136

Additional titles in the *Thirty Days with a Great Spiritual Teacher* series

GOD AWAITS YOU
Based on the Classic Spirituality of *Meister Eckhart*

LET NOTHING DISTURB YOU
A Journey to the Center of the Soul with *Teresa of Avila*

PEACE OF HEART
Based on the Life and Teachings of *Francis of Assisi*

SIMPLY SURRENDER
Based on the Little Way of *Thérèse of Lisieux*

TRUE SERENITY
Based on Thomas A Kempis' *The Imitation of Christ*

YOU SHALL NOT WANT
A Spiritual Journey Based on *The Psalms*

WHERE ONLY LOVE CAN GO
A Journey of the Soul into *The Cloud of Unknowing*

Future titles in the series will focus on authors and classic works such as Hildegard of Bingen, John of the Cross, Catherine of Siena, Brother Lawrence, and others.

30 Days with a Great Spiritual Teacher

All Will Be Well

Based on the Classic Spirituality of

Julian of Norwich

Richard Chilson

AVE MARIA PRESS Notre Dame , Indiana 46556

Richard Chilson is the author of over a dozen books on Catholicism and world religions. He currently serves as chaplain at the University of California at Berkeley.

First printing, July, 1995
Third printing, October, 1999
32,000 copies in print

The writings of Julian of Norwich included in this book are paraphrased from *Showings*, sometimes called *Revelations of Divine Love*, first published in the Fourteenth Century.

Copyright © 1995 Quest Associates

All rights reserved. No part of this book may be used or reproduced in any manner whatsoever, except in the case of brief excerpts in the context of reviews, without written permission of the publisher, Ave Maria Press, Inc., P.O. Box 428, Notre Dame, Indiana 46556.

International Standard Book Number: 0-87793-563-7

Library of Congress Card Number: 95-77233

Cover and text design by Elizabeth J. French

Printed and bound in the United States of America

Contents

Julian of Norwich and Showings ◆ 7
How to Pray This Book ◆ 23
Thirty Days With Julian of Norwich ◆ 33
One Final Word ◆ 215

Would you discern your Lord's meaning in this thing?
Know it well.
Love was his meaning.
Who showed it to you? Love.
What did he show you? Love.
Why did he show it? For love.
Grasp hold of this
and you will grow in deeper knowledge of love.
But nothing else will you ever know—ever!

—Julian of Norwich

Julian of Norwich

and Showings

(Revelations of Divine Love)

For a mystic of such a great influence, we know precious little about Julian of Norwich. We do not even know whether Julian was her name. For she was an anchoress whose house was attached to the church of St. Julian in Norwich—whether she too was named Julian is anyone's guess. She lived in the late fourteenth century and is the first woman writer in English whose work survives. A contemporary of Chaucer, her prose is treasured for its grace and lucidity.

She has left us but one work, although in two versions. Known as the *Showings* it describes visions which she had received from God and plumbs the meaning of these revelations. The major vision occurred in May 1373 and the first version, the shorter work was written soon after that. The second and longer version was not written until some twenty years later. It expands upon the earlier work and delves more into the meaning of the visions. Our excerpts are drawn mostly from the expanded version.

But before proceeding, it might be well for us to have some idea of Julian's world. Although she was a recluse, she was not entirely apart from the world. She lived sealed in a cottage joined to the church in the city of Norwich. The modern fiction is that an anchorite was walled into a tiny church-alcove with barely room for a prie-dieu and hard bed. Julian would probably have had a suite of rooms as well as a walled garden. Solitaries were even allowed to have cattle and property. They also had guests. The life was simple with much of it devoted to prayer and contemplation, but it was not the cruel torture we might imagine.

A main road passed right outside her house and Julian gave spiritual direction and advice to the many people who sought her out. One of these was Margery Kempe, who while certainly not of Julian's sanctity, has entered history for writing the first women's biography in English. Nor was Julian entirely alone within her cottage. She would have had a maid (we know the names of two of them). And she may have had pets.

Norwich was a busy port in her time. And a time of trouble it was. The plague swept through the city repeatedly. Disease and bad weather produced famine. The church itself was wracked by the

Great Schism with two competing popes. The Hundred Years War was raging. And when John Wycliffe and his followers called for reform in the church, they were burned as heretics. Some of them would have been led along the road in front of Julian's retreat on the way to their death. Julian, walled up though she was, was not sitting in an ivory tower.

Nor was she isolated from the learning of her time. An Augustinian friary was across the street from her house and it would have been natural for her to borrow books and engage in conversation with the friars. There were women's communities in the area as well. In fact there might even have been a group known as Beguines—a women's movement that inspired reform in the church.

Julian sets her vision in context when she reports that she had asked three boons of God. First, she wishes to remember Christ's passion in a special way. She does not ask to suffer as he suffered, but rather to enter into the feelings of a bystander. Second, she wanted to suffer from an illness so great that she and those around her would think it was mortal. By doing so, and coming through it, she felt that she would pass over and be able to devote herself entirely to the glory of God. Finally she wished for three wounds: "The wound of contrition, the wound of compassion, and the wound of longing with my will for God."

These wishes were granted. Julian speaks of her illness throughout *Showings*. And she is granted a vision of Christ's passion which she describes vividly and eloquently. The three wounds give her the grace to share her revelation with others.

As Julian reflects upon her experiences over the years she becomes more and more willing to trust them and to use them almost as a sacred text along with the scriptures. Like many mystics her direct experience of God allows her to correct the dominant spirituality of her day and align the Christian community more with the original revelation of Jesus.

And even to today's reader Julian provides a wonderful, joyous corrective to much of Christianity. While many Christians might fit into what William James called the unhealthy soul—seeing the world and God primarily in terms of sin and judgment—Julian is an example of the healthy soul. For her love and joy are paramount in the experience of God. If you are approaching Julian from a background of puritanical Christianity, whether Protestant or Catholic, bear in mind that shocking as some of her images and thoughts are, she is quite within the Catholic tradition.

Julian's great illness was a major conversion experience. All Christian conversion is primarily imaged by death-resurrection. It begins with baptism, but hopefully continues throughout one's life. Any death experience is a stripping away, a dying to one's past. The resurrection out of death is a new beginning, and new beginnings are uncluttered. The death experience forces one to sort out the essential from the expendable. People confronting life-threatening illness often undergo deep conversion experiences. They realize their time is precious. If they want to do something, they had better do it now.

One could certainly maintain that Christian teaching in Julian's day and even in our own is hardly uncluttered. Christians have so fussed over and nuanced the good news that sometimes it is difficult to see what is so liberating about the gospel. The liberation comes in resurrection. And Julian's encounter with God puts things in perspective for her.

In the shorter version of the text her revelations seem quite reserved and unassuming. But by the time of the final text she is willing to put them on a level with scripture. She trusts that God is truly revealing himself to her. This leads her not to contradict church teaching, but to refocus the emphasis upon salvation and love rather than law and justice.

What does Julian offer the modern reader? First she adds her voice to the growing reexamination of patriarchal images of God. She does not deny traditional teaching but she adds the dimension of Mother and specifically applies it to Jesus. Christ nourishes us from his breasts. This metaphor is not without precedent. Jesus himself used feminine imagery in speaking of the kingdom of God—a woman baking bread, a widow looking for a coin. He even referred to himself as a hen who would gather her chicks under her wing. Patriarchal Christianity has not mined these metaphors but

Julian exalts the feminine as a necessary corrective.

Even when she speaks of God's masculinity, she adds an important image. She tells us of Christ's immense courtesy. Of course in her day courtesy—or how to act at court—was of tremendous importance. Yet only Julian applies this virtue to God. Today many see God as almighty judge or awesome king. And so God is. But without this incredible courtesy God becomes the tyrant of tyrants. Surely Jesus refutes such an assumption. God's courtesy makes God supremely respectful of us, patient with our failings, honoring of our freedom. It makes God incredibly appealing and close as well. How can we not love a God who is so solicitous of us?

Julian's teaching on sin is also important today. For many,

Christianity spends too much effort pondering sin. Sin almost seems more significant than grace. Although they would be loath to admit it, these Christians display an obsession with sin that suggests it abounds more than grace.

While sin is certainly real for Julian, it is not the preeminent reality. She is conscious of it primarily in herself. Over and over she applies the words from her revelation that somehow in the mystery of God, "All will be well." She even wrestles with the church's teaching on the damned, and, while not denying that possibility, trusts that Christ has all things in hand and will bring good out of all things.

Again this is solid Catholic teaching. The church merely affirms that there must be the possibility of hell to allow for human freedom. God will make no one enter the kingdom against their will. But we do not have to believe that anyone has ever made the choice of denying the power of love.

Perhaps the most striking image in Julian is one that we have to read between the lines to see. She tells us to think of ourselves as infants. When we have soiled ourselves we do not descend into a pit of shame and blame. No, we run immediately to our mother who welcomes us, changes our diaper, hugs, and kisses us and the sends us on our way. It is a humiliating image for an adult, but in that humility lies its power to reveal God's love to us.

Finally Julian gives us the gift of joy. So much Christianity wears a gloomy, sour face. Yet the gospel is good news. God loves us to the extent of stooping into a human form and dying for us. Wake up to the beauty and the love which oozes out of every moment in all creation! Julian may have been an anchoress shut up in a cottage, but that cottage opened upon a walled garden as well as a busy street. The love of creation and human society fills her work. Her joy is contagious; it overflows. We can certainly profit from so gracious and ecstatic a voice in our anxious age.

Our selections are all drawn from the longer second version of the *Showings*. We have not included any of the revelations themselves, but rather concentrate on the meaning Julian drew from them. This is not a translation but rather a paraphrase of her work.

We have focused upon those aspects of her thought relevant to anyone interested in the spiritual life. Institutional references to church, dogma, and sacraments are minimized, and, although she understood her original readers to be baptized Christians, we have extended that audience to include all who seek love and life. This book is a threshold inviting us to become acquainted with one of the great mystics and writers of English. Hopefully it will inspire you to go on to encounter her first hand.

How to Pray This Book

The purpose of this book is to open a gate for you, to make accessible the spiritual experience and wisdom of one of the world's great spiritual teachers, Julian of Norwich.

This is not a book for mere reading. It invites you to meditate and pray its words on a daily basis over a period of thirty days.

It is a handbook for a spiritual journey.

Before you read the "rules" for taking this spiritual journey, remember that this book is meant to free your spirit, not confine it. If on any day the meditation does not resonate well for you, turn elsewhere to find a passage which seems to best fit the spirit of your day and your soul. Don't hesitate to repeat a day as often as you like until you feel that you have discovered what the Spirit, through the words of the author, has to say to your spirit.

Here are suggestions on one way to use this book as a cornerstone of your prayers.

As Your Day Begins

As the day begins set aside a quiet moment in a quiet place to read the meditation suggested for that day.

The passage is short. It never runs more than a couple of hundred words, but it has been carefully selected to give a spiritual focus, a spiritual center to your whole day. It is designed to remind you as another day begins of your own existence at a spiritual level. It is meant to put you in the presence of the spiritual master who is your companion and teacher on this journey. But most of all the purpose of the passage is to remind you that at this moment and at every moment during this day you will be living and acting in the presence of a God who invites you continually, but quietly to live in and through him.

A word of advice: read slowly. Very slowly. The meditation has been broken down into sense lines to help you do just this. Don't read to get to the end, but to savor each part of the meditation. You never know what short phrase, what word, will trigger a response in your spirit. Give the words a chance. After all you are not just reading this passage, you are praying it. You are setting a mood of serenity for your whole day. What's the rush?

All Through Your Day

Immediately following the day's reading you will find a single sentence which we call a mantra, a word borrowed from the Hindu tradition.

This phrase is meant as a companion for your spirit as it moves through a busy day. Write it down on a 3"x 5" card or on the appropriate page of your daybook. Look at it as often as you can. Repeat it quietly to yourself and go on your way.

It is not meant to stop you in your tracks or to distract you from responsibilities, but simply, gently to remind you of the presence of God and your desire to respond to this presence.

As Your Day Is Ending

This is a time for letting go of the day. Find a quiet place and quiet your spirit. Breathe deeply. Inhale, exhale—slowly and deliberately, again and again until you feel your body let go of its tension.

You will find a series of questions designed to help you review your day in the light of the meditation. Answer them slowly, thoughtfully, without anxiety or stress. They are not a test but simply a method for concentrating the spiritual energy of your day as it comes to an end.

Now read the evening prayer slowly, phrase by phrase. You may recognize at once phrases taken from the meditation with which you began your day and the mantra that has accompanied you all through your day. In this way a simple evening prayer gathers together the spiritual character of the day that is now ending as it began—in the presence of God.

It is a time for summary and closure. Invite God to embrace you with love and to protect you through the night. Sleep well.

Some Other Ways to Use This Book

1. Use it anyway your spirit suggests. As mentioned earlier, skip a passage that doesn't resonate for you on a given day, or repeat for a second day or even several days a passage whose richness speaks to you. The truths of a spiritual life are not absorbed in a day, or for that matter, in a lifetime. So take your time. Be patient with the Lord. Be patient with yourself.

2. Take two passages and/or their mantras—the more contrasting the better—and "bang" them together. Spend time discovering how their similarities or differences illumine your path.

3. Start a spiritual journal to record and deepen your experience of this thirty-day journey. Using either the mantra or another phrase from the reading that appeals to you, write a spiritual

account of your day, a spiritual reflection. Create your own meditation.

4. Join the millions who are seeking to deepen their spiritual life by joining with others to form small groups. More and more people are doing just this to aid and support each other in their mutual spiritual quest. Meet once a week, or at least every other week, to discuss and pray about one of the meditations. There are many books and guides available to help you make such a group effective.

Thirty Days with Julian of Norwich

Day One

My Day Begins

And God showed me a little thing,
in the palm of my hand,
round like a ball,
no bigger than a hazelnut.
I gazed at it, puzzling at what it might be.
And God said to me,
"It is all of creation."
I was amazed that it could last
and did not suddenly disintegrate

and fall into nothingness,
for it was so tiny.
And again God spoke to me,
"It lasts, both now and forever,
because I cherish it."
And I understood that everything has its being
owing to God's care and love.
We need to realize the insignificance of creation
and see it for the emptiness it is
before we can embrace the uncreated God in love.
We will find no rest for our heart or spirit
as long as we seek it in insignificant things
which cannot satisfy us,
rather than in God
who is omnipotent, omniscient, and beneficent.
He is our true repose.

And he desires to be known
and is pleased that we should rest in him.
For nothing less than him can satisfy us.
We cannot rest
until we are detached from all that is created.
When we have done so
for love of God who is all,
only then are we able to enjoy spiritual rest.

All Through the Day

Nothing less than God can satisfy us.

My Day Is Ending

Take the image of the hazel nut.

What incidents in your life today seem as small and insignificant as this hazel nut?

Imagine feeling God's concern and love for you
in these small things.
What small things distracted you
from the experience of God's love today?

When did you remember to rest in God today?

Night Prayer

Out of your goodness, Lord,
give me yourself,
for you are sufficient for me,
and I can ask for nothing which is less
which can render you full worship.
And if I ask anything less,
I am constantly lacking;
only in you do I possess everything.

Day Two

My Day Begins

For just as our body is clothed in garments,
our flesh enclosed by our skin,
our bones wrapped in flesh,
our heart centered in our body;
so are we, spirit and flesh,
clothed head to toe in the goodness of God.
But this metaphor hardly does justice,
for all these things will decline and wear out,
but God's goodness is everlasting,

and it is incomparably nearer us than our very flesh.
Our Beloved wishes that our spirit might cling to him
with all our strength,
and never let go of his goodness.
No mere creature can ever imagine
just how dearly, sweetly, and tenderly
our Creator loves us.
So with his grace and aid
let us spiritually rest in contemplation,
forever marveling
at the high, surpassing, single-minded,
immeasurable love
which our good Lord extends to us.
Doing so, we can dare ask our lover
for whatever we wish,
because by its nature our will seeks only God.

And God in turn desires only us.
And never can we stop
desiring and longing
until he is ours in the fullness of bliss.
Above all else,
this fond gazing upon our Creator
makes us aware of our own insignificance,
fills us with awe, humility,
and abounding love for our neighbor.

All Through the Day

So are we spirit and flesh,
clothed head to toe
in the goodness of God.

My Day Is Ending

What was your humblest need today?
Did you sense God's presence there?
Remember this need
and sense God's presence and love there now.
How and when did you sense yourself clad and enclosed
in God's goodness today?

Spend a few moments now in contemplation:
God is adhering to you
and you, in turn, adhere to God.

Night Prayer

Gentlest God,
clasp me in your arms.
Show me your love
for the least of me
and inspire me in turn to such love
that you become all my will,
all my love,
and the fullness of my joy.

Day Three

My Day Begins

Our Lord desires
that our spirit be truly turned to gaze upon him
and upon all his glorious creation,
for it is exceedingly good.
And his judgments are sweet and comforting,
and bring our spirit to rest.
Thus we turn from scrutinizing our own blind actions
toward the delightfulness of God.

For we consider some actions good
and others wrong,
but God does not look upon them so:
for God has made all things,
so all that is done
is in some way God's doing.
For it is easy to see
that the best actions are well done,
but the smallest actions also share this character,
because all things
have been accomplished
according to the nature and plan
ordered by God from the beginning.
No one acts but God.
God never changes his mind in anything,
and never will.

Nothing in creation
was unknown by him from the beginning.
All was set in order before anything was made.
Nothing will fail in its design,
for all is abundantly good.
So the Trinity is entirely pleased with all its works.
Behold, I am God.
Behold, I am in all things.
Behold, I accomplish all things.
Behold, I never withdraw my arms from my work.
Behold, I never fail to guide all things
toward the purpose for which I created them,
before time began,
with the strength, wisdom, and love
with which I created all.
So how can anything go wrong?

All Through the Day

Behold, I never withdraw my arms from my work.

My Day Is Ending

Recall something today
which you thought went poorly at the time.
In your imagination now picture it ultimately going well,
as it is in God's care.
Is there something from your past
which you felt at one time to be a failure
but which you now can see
God was working towards a good end?
What do you think failed for you today?
Take it to God in prayer.
Ask God to comfort you in the rightness of what happened.
Be relaxed in this meditation;
don't push too hard. Let God comfort you.

Night Prayer

Most wonderful Lover.
Help me to see that you are God.
To see how you are in all things.
To have confidence that you do all things.
To trust that you never abandon your work.
Guide me and all creation to that end
you have ordained for us, before time began.
I have confidence you will do so
with the same power, wisdom, and love
with which you made us.
Convince us more deeply
that nothing in you can be amiss.

Day Four

My Day Begins

Now our Lord reminded me
of the desire for him I had earlier.
I saw that nothing stood in my way but sin,
and I realized that this is the same for all of us,
and I thought that if there were no sin,
we would all be pure and akin to our Lord
just as we had been created.
But in my vision
Jesus informed me of everything necessary

for me to know,
and he told me:
Sin is necessary,
but everything will turn out for the good,
and all will be well,
and everything will be well.
By the simple word, "sin"
God reminded me of all that is not good
and of the suffering and grief of all creation,
and above all of the utter shame and sacrifice
he endured for our salvation.
We have all suffered woe and sorrow
as we follow our master Jesus,
and we shall do so until we are utterly purified.
I did not see sin itself,
for it has no real substance,

it is not real;
it can be known only by the suffering it causes,
and even that pain lasts but a while.
And during the woe
we might take consolation in our Lord's suffering.
And out of his tender love he consoles us, saying:
True, sin caused this pain, but all will be well.
In his voice I never hear a hint of blame,
and since we who are guilty are not blamed,
why should we in turn blame God?

All Through the Day

Sin is necessary, but all will be well.

My Day Is Ending

What in your day might you look at as sin,
as something that hindered your relation to God?
Imagine how it might work out well in the end
following Julian's insight.
Consider some of the sins of our world
such as war and pollution.
How might these sins draw us closer to God?
How might they awaken us to our precarious condition
and help us to turn toward God?
Can you see the sins and failings of this day as a lack?
Julian says it has no kind of substance.
How can you see this in your own sins and failings?

Night Prayer

God our Comforter,
show me how you guide me through my life
not only in my joys and virtues
but even when I choose wrong
and am weak.
Give us hope
that in the midst of denial and darkness
your love still holds us readily and sweetly,
guiding us home.

Day Five

My Day Begins

And I beheld Christ's mercy upon us
on account of our sin,
and just as previously,
I was filled with sorrow and pity
because of Christ's suffering,
so now I was moved with compassion
on behalf of my neighbors,
the servants of God,
who are all greatly loved and saved.

For our community is shaken
by grief, anguish, and woe,
as you would shake a rag in the wind.
And I began to understand
how our Lord could rejoice
with sympathy and compassion
over the afflictions of his people;
and he visits something upon each one he loves,
in order to bring us to happiness.
And although this thing carries no blame in his eyes,
yet because of it we are scorned and rejected by the world.
Jesus wishes us to realize
that it will be converted to our glory and benefit
by the strength of his suffering.
Nor do we endure distress alone,
but are united to him.

We behold in him the ground of our being.
And we realize that his suffering and affliction
so far surpass anything we might endure
that we cannot fully comprehend it.
When we come to see this
we will stop weeping and lamenting
our own sufferings;
we begin to understand
that our sufferings are well deserved,
but his love always excuses us.
Out of his great courtesy
he never censures us,
but instead looks upon us
with compassion and sympathy,
seeing us as righteous children without guilt.

All Through the Day

Out of his great courtesy
he never censures us.

My Day Is Ending

Call to mind Christ's passion
and unite it in your imagination
with any pain which you have suffered today.
Imagine these together
working for the healing of the world.
Who do you flow out towards with compassion
in their pain?
Call them to mind now
and unite them also
in the passion of Christ and your own suffering.
Recall any defects
you may have experienced during the day
and imagine them of no account in Christ's sight.

Let them go.
Drop them into the passion of Christ.

Night Prayer

Most courteous Lord,
may my sins, defects and sufferings
be joined to your passion.
Help me to bear
misunderstanding, prejudice and rejection,
knowing they will be healed.
Give me faith
that all pains will be turned to our honor and profit
and will culminate in bliss and joy.

Day Six

My Day Begins

God wants us to be enfolded in repose and peace.
Only then shall Christ's spiritual thirst be satisfied.
This is his thirst:
his desire to love us
which shall continue until the last day,
when we shall be completely gathered
into his joy and happiness.
He yearns to integrate us into himself in bliss.
For we are not yet as fully immersed in him

as we shall be.
Christ Jesus is both human and divine.
Because he is divine, he is supreme happiness,
so he was from the beginning,
so shall he be until the ending.
This happiness can neither increase or diminish.
Because he is human,
he, though divine,
suffered and died out of love to bring us to bliss.
And he takes joy in these deeds of his humanity.
For he told me:
It gives me joy, bliss, and eternal delight
to have suffered for you.
This is the satisfaction he receives from his work.
As Christ is our head,
he is glorious and invincible.

And as he is the body in which we are all conjoined,
he is not yet wholly glorified or invincible.
He still carries that same thirst
which he had upon the cross.
And he shall continue to suffer it
until the last spirit has been brought up to join him.
Because he yearns for us, we in turn ache for him,
and no one comes to bliss without such an ache.
This thirst springs from God's eternal goodness
just as compassion does.
So he is compassionate towards us
and desires to possess us.
But his wisdom and love
will not allow the end to come
before the time is ripe.

All Through the Day

Because he yearns for us,
we in turn ache for him,
and no one comes to bliss without it.

My Day Is Ending

Recall times during this day
when you felt some yearning for wholeness.
Were you able to connect your own yearning
with that of God yearning for you in turn?
Were there any moments of peace and rest for you today?
Recall them now
and spend a few moments savoring them.
See if in your recollection
you can make them even more peaceful.
And imagine as well
how much more peaceful you might be in the future.
Take time to relax and enjoy this meditation.

Night Prayer

Dear Lord,
thank you for the glimpses of peace and rest
you have provided today.
Help me to know your longing for me,
and aid my desire to turn to you above all else.
In my sorrow
give me assurance that you suffer with me
and that eventually we shall be together
in complete happiness.

Day Seven

My Day Begins

On one occasion our good Lord told me:
every kind of thing will be all right.
He desires us to understand
that not only does he concern himself
with great and noble things,
but equally with small and simple things.
We too should realize
that the smallest thing will not be forgotten.
Now there are many acts committed

which to us seem so evil and so harmful
that we despair of any good resulting from them.
While we are in sorrow and mourning concerning these,
we cannot relax
in God's exalted and wondrous wisdom.
For our reason is now so blinded, weak, and ignorant
that we cannot see
the Trinity's strength and goodness.
So God tells us:
You will yourself behold that all will be well.
It is as though he were telling us:
Take it now in faith and trust,
and in the end you will see truly, in all fullness and joy.
The Trinity will accomplish an action on the last day;
what it will be and how it will be accomplished
no creature lower than Christ knows,

and so shall it remain veiled
until the act is accomplished.
And he wishes us to know this
so that our spirits
might be surrendered peacefully into his love,
and we might then ignore
every disturbance
which thwarts our true rejoicing in God.

All Through the Day

The smallest thing will not be forgotten.

My Day Is Ending

Think of a time today
when you forgot today's mantra,
when you felt forgotten.
In memory now bring it to today's phrase
and sit with it knowing that God holds all in love.
Is there something that happened today
which strikes you as useless, counterproductive,
no good can come of it?
Remember it now and in faith bring it to God.
Let God assure you of its hidden significance.
Can you remember some incident from the past
which at the time you felt to be not good or even evil,
but which now you can see as a stepping stone
along your spiritual journey?

Night Prayer

Dear Lord,
help me to trust in your wisdom
that nothing is forgotten.
Give me the strength to meet the events of my life
believing that in you all will be revealed
and everything made well.
Help me to surrender my anxiety
so that my spirit might have ease
and be at peace
in love.

Day Eight

My Day Begins

This is the great act
intended by our Lord God from eternity,
treasured and hidden in his heart,
known only to himself.
By this act he will make all things well.
For just as the blessed Trinity
made everything from nothing,
just so will the same Trinity
make everything wrong to be well.

And I was overcome with wonder at this:
our faith is grounded in God's word,
and whoever believes in that word
will be preserved completely.
Now holy doctrine tells us
that many creatures will be damned.
And if this is true
it seemed impossible to me
that everything should be well,
as our Lord had shown me by revelation.

And in regard to this
I had no other answer but this:
"What is impossible for you
is not impossible for me.
I shall honor my word in everything,

and I shall make everything well."

So I was instructed by God's grace
to hold steadfastly to the faith,
and at the same time
to believe firmly
that everything will turn out for the best.
For this is the great action
which our Lord will accomplish,
and in this action he will keep his word entirely.
And what is not well
shall be made well.

All Through the Day

What is impossible for you is not so for me.

My Day Is Ending

What seemed most impossible today?
Bring it to God now in prayer
and surrender it to his wisdom.
Were there times today you were tempted
or did not trust that all will be well?
Did you bring the mantra into the situation?
Did you forget about the reading entirely?
Do not enter into judgment.
Simply observe how you acted
—no blame, no regret,
just be curious about how you dealt with the moment.

Night Prayer

Dear Lord,
thank you for sharing your plan with us
that you will keep your word in everything.
Help me to trust in your words
and to let go of things
that are beyond me.
May I find the faith
to surrender the impossible to you
so that I have more time to enjoy
the many beauties
with which you visit me.

Day Nine

My Day Begins

Sin is the sharpest scourge
which can strike anyone's spirit.
This scourge wears down both man and woman,
making them loathsome in their own sight,
and it is not long
till they consider themselves suited only to hell,
until the Holy Spirit's touch
moves them to contrition

and turns bitterness into hope in God's mercy.
Then the Spirit begins to heal the wounds,
revive the spirit,
and return the person to life.
Dearly does our Lord protect us in his loving care
when we seem to be almost forsaken
and cast away on account of our sin.
And indeed we deserve as much.
Yet because of the humility we acquire in this fashion
we are raised high in God's sight through his grace.
Contrition makes us clean,
compassion renders us ready,
and desire for God makes us worthy.
So all shame is transformed into joy and glory.
For our courteous Lord
does not wish his creatures to lose hope

even if they fall frequently and grievously;
for our failure does not prevent him loving us.
Peace and love are always present within us,
living and laboring,
but we unfortunately
do not always abide in peace and love.

All Through the Day

Our failure does not prevent him loving us.

My Day Is Ending

Can you remember instances in the past
when your own pain and awareness of your faults
have opened you up to compassion for others?
Relive that moment now through memory.
Recall a time today when peace and love
definitely did not seem present for you.
In your imagination relive this event
in the knowledge that God's peace and love
were truly present,
even though you were unaware of it.

Night Prayer

Courteous Lord Jesus,
help us to acknowledge and accept
all our failings, sins, and weaknesses,
trusting that you use them to our good
and through them draw us closer to you.
May our contrition make us clean,
may our compassion make us ready,
and may our longing for you make us worthy.
At all times preserve us in the knowledge
that your peace and love abide always in us,
living and working,
even when we have no feeling of peace or love.

Day Ten

My Day Begins

God wants us to understand prayer.
First, we must know through whom
and how our prayer begins;
so he told me:
"I am the foundation."
Second, he wishes to teach us how to pray best:
our will should be conformed joyfully to God's will.
Third, he desires us
to know the fruit and outcome of our prayer:

to be united and similar to our Lord in all things.
God intends our prayer and trust to be magnanimous.
If we do not trust as much as we pray,
we do not honor God fully,
and we place obstacles in our path.
This happens because we do not realize
that God himself is the ground of our praying.
Our very ability to pray is a gift of his loving grace.
We cannot ask for mercy and grace
unless they have first been extended to us.
Sometimes, it seems after praying a long time
we have received no answer.
We should not let this disturb us.
God simply wishes
we should wait for a more suitable time,
or more grace, or a better gift.

Furthermore,
just as we experience God drawing us to him,
so we should pray that we be drawn toward him.
It is not sufficient to do one without the other.
If we pray, but do not see that God is at work,
we become dejected and downcast
and so do him no honor.
And if we see him at work, but do not pray,
we do less than our duty.
But to see that he works, and to pray that he works,
gives God worship and benefits us.
When we pray thus we will think we have done nothing.
But if we do what we can,
seeking mercy and grace,
we shall discover in him all that is deficient in us.

All Through the Day

You are the ground of my prayer.

My Day Is Ending

Look back over your day in terms of trust.
Were there times
when you felt able to trust God or another person?
Were there times when such trust was lacking?
Relive an incident now,
imagining a fullness of trust present.
How does it change the experience?
Spend some time contemplating God
as the very foundation from which prayer springs.
Visualize prayer flowing from this ground into you
and back to God.
When you pray in the future

you might begin your prayer with this short visualization; use it as a gateway into prayer.

Night Prayer

Lord, teach me to pray
and trust more fully in you.
Give me assurance
that you are with me always,
and teach me to be content
with the plan you have for me
and all your creatures.

Day Eleven

My Day Begins

In his merciful way
our good Lord always leads us
as long as we inhabit this impermanent life.
And I saw no anger other than humanity's,
and God forgives us that,
for anger is no more
than perverse opposition to peace and love.
It arises from a lack of strength,
or wisdom, or goodness.

And this failure lies in ourselves
rather than in God.
Our sin and desperation
generate in us a wrath
and a continual opposition to peace and love.
But the ground of mercy is love,
and the ministry of mercy is to preserve us in love.
For mercy works in love,
with generosity, compassion, and sweetness.
And mercy labors within us,
preserving us, and converting everything to the good.
Through love mercy allows us to fail,
at least in part,
and to the extent we fail, we fall;
to the extent we fall, we die.
For we die without fail

when we no longer see and feel God,
who is life.
Our failure is frightful,
our falling inglorious,
our dying wretched.
Yet never does love's compassionate eye turn from us,
nor the operation of mercy cease.

All Through the Day

Never
does love's compassionate eye
turn from us.

My Day Is Ending

Review your day
and focus particularly upon moments of anger.
Do not condemn yourself for the anger,
but with curiosity ask yourself
whether the anger could have been caused
by a lack of power, wisdom, or goodness.
Bring God's mercy to your moments of anger.
Let the mercy touch each moment.
There is no need to force a healing.
Simply allow the mercy to touch each moment of anger.
Let what happens or does not happen simply be.
Have no goal in this exercise except the process itself.

Night Prayer

Loving Father,
I bring to you all my faults
and especially my wrath.
I see my anger leads to a dreadful failing,
a shameful falling,
and a sorrowful dying.
But in this dying
I trust your mercy
continually at work protecting me
even against myself,
and turning everything to good for us.

Day Twelve

My Day Begins

And I saw in my visions
that in truth
God, as far as he is concerned,
never has to forgive us,
because he is incapable of becoming angry!
For all life is founded in love
and without that love life is impossible.
Wrath and amity are inherently opposed.
And since God relieves and takes away our anger,

by which he humbles and tames us,
he himself must surely be loving, humble, and gentle,
and so quite the opposite of angry.
We shall not be safe and blessed
until we abide in peace and love:
this is what salvation means.
And I beheld God as our genuine peace;
he is our protector when we ourselves are disturbed,
and he continually labors to bring us to rest.
But we shall not experience this peace
until we are wholly content with God,
and at love and peace
with both self and neighbor.
For contention is the cause of all our trouble and woe;
and our Lord Jesus
lifts them from us

and raises them up,
where they become
more sweet and pleasurable
than heart can think or tongue tell.
And when we come home,
we shall find them there,
turned entirely into beauty and love.

All Through the Day

All life is founded in love
and without that love
life is impossible.

My Day Is Ending

Recollect some moments of peace in your life today.
Let them expand in your imagination.
Be aware of that peace as a resting in God.

Can you remember moments of contrariness today?
How did things progress from them?
Did they lead to tribulation and woe,
or did they lead to something else?
How did you respond to your contrariness?
Do not judge yourself.
Just be curious as to how you acted and what resulted.

Night Prayer

Dear God,
in your endless friendship
thank you for being patient with me.
Help me to be patient with myself.
Let me see my contrariness
as leading me closer to your love and peace.
Thank you for your presence
in the midst of my disquiet
which I know will be turned into true beauty
and endless love.

Day Thirteen

My Day Begins

Our Father's pity and compassion were for Adam,
his loved creature, when he fell.
His joy and happiness were for his dearly loved Son,
who is equal with the Father.
The merciful gaze of his face
ranged over all the world,
and descended with Adam into hell,
and this unceasing compassion
preserved Adam from eternal death.

This same mercy and compassion abide with us
until we are drawn up to heaven.
But we are blinded in this life,
and cannot behold God, our Father, as God is.
And when out of his kindness
he desires to show himself to us,
he shows himself in great simplicity,
as a human being.
However I saw quite clearly
that we should not assume
that the Father is a creature.
But his sitting on the bare and wasted earth
means this: God made our spirit
to be his own city and resting place.
Of all creation
this is most pleasing to him.

And when we had fallen into grief and suffering,
we were not suited to that noble office.
But our kind Father
would not ready any other place to dwell,
but, instead, sat upon the ground,
waiting for humanity,
itself mixed with clay,
until such time as through grace,
his beloved Son had restored to this city
its noble beauty
through his tremendous labor.

All Through the Day

The merciful gaze of his face
ranged over all the world.

My Day Is Ending

God reveals himself to us in the human face and form.
How did you catch a sense of God today
in the people you met?

Call up the image of God,
sitting on the barren ground in exile
awaiting Christ to bring back his city—our spirit.
Join with the longing, passion, and love of God
in this exile.
Simply remain with this image in your heart for a time.
Let it reveal God's endless love for humanity
and for you in particular.

Night Prayer

Dearest friend,
help me sense your longing for me.
May your exile from the human spirit
inspire in me an equal desire
for your presence within me.
And I give thanks for Jesus, your Son,
who by his hard work
has brought back your city, my spirit,
into its noble place of beauty.

Day Fourteen

My Day Begins

Our life in this world
consists of a wondrous mixture of good and bad.
We contain within us
both our risen Lord Jesus Christ,
as well as the misery and woe of Adam's sin.
Protected by Christ, although dying,
we are touched by his grace
and raised to hope of salvation.
Afflicted by Adam's fall,

as well as our own sinfulness and woe,
we feel so benighted and blinded
that we can scarcely find any comfort.
But in our hearts
we trust in God,
and hope in his mercy and grace;
for they are truly at work in us.
And our good God opens the eye of our understanding
so that we might see,
sometimes more, sometimes less,
according to the ability God gives us to receive it.
Now we are raised up to one,
now allowed to fall to the other.
And this fluctuation is so confusing
that we hardly know where we stand,
whether we consider ourselves or our fellows.

But what a marvelous confusion!
And it continues throughout our life.
But God wants us to trust that he is always with us.
He accompanies us in three ways:
in heaven, where in his rising he raises us up with him;
on earth, where he leads us day by day;
and in our innermost being,
where he constantly dwells to guide and preserve us.
And this is our comfort,
that we know in faith
that Christ is constantly with us,
so that we never succumb to the pain and woe,
but always hope for another glimpse of his presence.

All Through the Day

God wants us to trust
that he is always with us.

My Day Is Ending

Did you experience a marvelous mixture
of both well-being and woe today?
Recall it to mind now.
If you have no experience from today, recall some past event.
This is not a pleasant experience, but it is life.
Sense in the experience a faith
that all is truly in God's hands and power.
If you experienced today
the dark and blindness Julian speaks of,
recall that event now
and see whether you were able to wait for God then,
or, if you can re-imagine the event now,
place at the center a waiting for God.

Night Prayer

Jesus, my protector,
hear my complaints, my pains, my woes.
Show yourself to me in my darkness.
Increase my hope and trust in you.
Help me sense and feel your presence
in my confusion and blindness.
Give me confidence
that through your cross
this unpalatable mixture will work to my good.

Day Fifteen

My Day Begins

Our spirit is made by God,
but it is made of nothing that is created.
This is how it is:
when God made our body,
he took the dirt of the earth,
which is substance mixed with all sorts of earthly things,
and from this he created our body.
But when God went to create our spirit,
he took nothing;

he simply created it.
Thus is created nature truly joined to God, its maker,
who is essential nature and uncreated.
Consequently nothing at all
can come between God and our spirit.
And by this eternal love
our spirit is preserved whole.
In this eternal love
God guides and protects us,
and we shall never be lost,
for God desires us to understand
that the spirit is alive,
and his goodness and grace assure us
that this life will last forever,
loving him, thanking him, praising him.
And just as we were made for eternity,

so we are valued and enclosed in God,
known and loved from before time began.
So God desires us to know
that humanity is the best creature ever made,
and our complete expression and model
is the blessed spirit of Christ.
In addition, he desires us to know
that our beloved spirit
was wondrously knitted to him
in its creation
by a union so skillful and strong
that we are joined in God
and made holy forever.

All Through the Day

Nothing at all
can come between God
and our spirit.

My Day Is Ending

Can you recall any moments today
when you felt led and protected by God?
Did you experience this at the time?
Can you see it as so now?
Look back over your day
and see it completely bathed in God's love.
Include especially moments
when you may have felt far from such love.
Re-imagine them now
as Julian encourages us to do.

Night Prayer

Beloved One,
thank you for calling me into being
and holding me in your love.
Help me to feel how preciously
I am knitted to you.
Make me aware of the knot of love
that ties you to me,
so that I may courageously do your will.

Day Sixteen

My Day Begins

Because of God's great love for humanity
he does not make a distinction in love
between Christ and the least creature.
It is easy enough to believe
that the blessed Spirit of Christ
is high in the glorious Godhead;
but, as I have seen,
where the blessed Spirit of Christ dwells,
there dwell in him the spirits of all who will be saved.

So let us rejoice greatly
that God dwells within us;
and let us even more rejoice
that we dwell within God.
For our spirit is made to be God's resting place,
and our spirit's rest is in God
who is unmade.
Great it is to know in our heart
that God, who is our Maker,
rests in our spirit,
but far greater is it to know in our heart,
that our spirit, which is made,
rests in essence in God
and by that substance, God,
we are who we are!
And I beheld no difference

between God and our substance.
All was God, as it were;
yet I knew that our substance is in God.
In other words,
God is God,
and we are creatures in God.

All Through the Day

Our spirit is made
to be God's resting place.

My Day Is Ending

Julian says that "God dwells in our soul",
and also that "our soul dwells in God."
Take each phrase in turn
and look back over your day recalling times
when one or the other described your experience.
What is your experience?
God makes no distinction between Christ
and the least soul.
Re-imagine your day now
and see everyone who was with you in this day
caught up in the same love of Christ.
Especially focus upon people

whom you might be tempted to call least,
those who do not have an easy entry
to your own love and compassion.

Night Prayer

Beloved Friend,
I rejoice in your intimacy with me.
Remove all the barriers that stand between us.
I welcome you into my heart;
let me make you at home there.
And let me see all other creatures joined together
in our love and intimacy.

Day Seventeen

My Day Begins

I saw with utter certainty
that it is faster and easier for us to come to know God
than to know our own spirit.
For our spirit is so deeply set in God
and so endlessly valued
that we cannot hope to know it
until we first know God, our Creator,
to whom we are united.
God is nearer us than our own spirit.

For God is the ground upon which we stand,
and God is the means
by which our essence and sensuality
are united in such a way
that we may never be separated.
Our spirit dwells in God as its true rest,
and stands in God as its true strength,
and is rooted in God as its eternal love.
So if we wish to come to know our own spirit,
if we wish to have communion with it,
we must seek it in God in whom it is enclosed.
With certainty I saw
that our longing will be accompanied by sorrow
until we are led so deeply into God
that we do indeed know our own spirit.
Our Lord himself leads us

into these lofty depths
with the same love by which he made us and saved us
by the mercy and grace of his death.
And we will never fully know God
until we come to know ourselves thoroughly.
For our spirit reaches its full flowering
when our sensuality has been lifted up
to the level of our essence
through the virtue of Christ's death,
enriched by the trials God sends upon us
in mercy and grace.

All Through the Day

God is nearer to us than our own spirit.

My Day Is Ending

Take a few moments to reflect on the mystery of yourself.
Julian says we cannot know our own soul
except through God.
How might knowing God as your true depth
change your self-image?
We tend to think of ourselves
as apart from others and God.
Spend some time contemplating Julian's vision
that God is the foundation upon which our soul stands.
God is closer to us than we are to ourselves.
How might such an understanding
influence your outlook and behavior?

Night Prayer

Courteous God,
be the foundation of my being.
May I sit in you in true rest,
stand in you in sure strength,
and be rooted in you in endless love.
Reveal yourself more to me
so that I may know my true nature better
and act as I truly am.

Day Eighteen

My Day Begins

As for our essence,
God created us so noble and rich
that we always work in his will and for his glory.
Indeed I saw that we are his beloved,
and that we do what pleases him,
continually, and without cease.
And we are able to do this
by the great wealth and nobility given our spirit
when it was infused into our body.

Through this union we are made sensual.
In our essence we lack nothing,
but in our sensuality we fail,
although God will make good this failing
through his mercy and grace,
richly flowing into us from God's innate goodness.
I saw that from the beginning
God knows fully all the works
which God has or will ever accomplish.
He created the human race out of love,
and out of love he willed to take on our human nature.
Faith is the next gift we receive,
and from faith all blessings flow.
Faith springs out of the riches
with which our essence endows our sensitive soul,
God's goodness working through mercy and grace

plants this faith in us, and plants us in faith.
From faith flow all good things
by which we are guided and saved.
The virtues
which God's goodness draws from our essence
are gifts of the Holy Spirit
who works through mercy
and restores through grace.
These virtues and gifts
are our treasure in Jesus Christ.
For in the Virgin's womb
when God united himself to our humanity,
he took also our sensuality.
And Christ who unites himself with everyone
is perfect humanity.

All Through the Day

We do what pleases him,
continually, and without cease.

My Day Is Ending

When today did you feel God's love?
When might it have helped you
to sense more keenly God's love for you?
What is your own view of your sensuality?
How have you experienced God in the sensual today?
Is your search for God limited to the intangible?
How might you find God
in touch? smell? taste? sight? sound?

Night Prayer

Constant Friend,
nearer than my very self.
Help me feel your pleasure in all your creation.
Restore and fill what I lack
by the operation of your mercy and grace,
plentifully flowing into me
from your own natural goodness.
In your kindness
show me how you have taken up my soul,
enclosed me entirely in yourself,
and united us forever in love.

Day Nineteen

My Day Begins

We are blessed through mercy and grace,
but we would be ignorant of this goodness
were it not opposed.
For evil was allowed to rise up against goodness,
and then mercy and grace rose up against evil
and turned it to the good.
It is God's wisdom to set good against evil.
So Jesus who sets good against evil is our Mother.
We owe him our very being

—the essence of motherhood,
and all the delightful protection that follows after.
For as surely as God is Father,
so surely is God also Mother,
and he shows this in all,
but particularly in these sweet words:

I am the strength and goodness of the father,
I am the wisdom of the mother,
I am light, grace, and lovely love,
I am Trinity and unity;
I am the innate goodness of every creature,
I draw you towards love,
I endow you with longing;
I am the endless completion of all desiring.
So Jesus is our true Mother by nature

because he has created us.
He is also our Mother by grace,
for he took our created nature upon himself.
All the lovely deeds and tender services of motherhood
may be seen in him.
And I came to understand
three ways of looking at the Motherhood of God:
first, our being is made,
second, in Christ our nature is educated,
and thus begins the motherhood of grace;
third, the motherhood of work flows out
covering all with that same grace,
whose length, breadth, height, and depth
is forever and ever.
And so is God's love.

All Through the Day

I draw you towards love
I endow you with longing.

My Day Is Ending

How have you loved God today?
How might you have loved God?
Consider how you have experienced God as Father today.
How have you encountered God as mother?
What difference does it make in
how you relate to God
when you consider God as mother?

Night Prayer

Dear God,
power and goodness of fatherhood,
wisdom of motherhood,
light and grace which is all blessed love,
Trinity and unity,
make me long for you
enable me to love you
inspire me to seek you
as the fulfilling of all true desires.

Day Twenty

My Day Begins

A mother's service
is the most intimate, willing, and dependable,
because it is the most natural,
as well as the most loving,
and certainly it is the truest service we know.
And the only one who can perform this service
to its fullest is our Lord Jesus.
We know that our own mother bore us
in suffering and death.

But what does our true Mother do?
Only he, all loving, bears us for joy and endless life.
So he carried us within himself in love and pain,
until the fullness of time came
when he suffered the sharpest thorns
and most daunting pains,
and then at the end he died.
And not even when this was over,
not even when we are carried to eternal bliss,
is his everlasting love content.
I saw this in his wondrous words of love:
If I could have suffered more,
I would have.
He can die no more,
but that does not stop him;
he longs to feed us,

an obligation of his motherly love for us.
The human mother suckles her child with her own milk,
but Mother Jesus nourishes us with himself,
with the utmost courtesy, in the blessed sacrament,
the priceless food of eternal life.
And through all the sacraments
he accompanies us upon our journey
with mercy and grace.
Our human mother may place us tenderly at her breast,
but Mother Jesus leads us into her breast
through the wound in her side,
where we glimpse both Godhead and heavenly joy
and are made certain
of eternal happiness.

All Through the Day

Mother Jesus nourishes us with himself.

My Day Is Ending

How have you experienced God as mother today?
Julian sees Jesus' passion
as the birth pangs of a mother.
How might God have suffered
so that you might be born this day?
How has Jesus nourished you today?
Looking back now.
Are there other places and ways
in which you might have eaten the food of Christ?

Night Prayer

Devoted Mother,
I thank you for rebirthing me to life.
I give thanks
for the food which is yourself
given as my daily bread.
You nourish me into health and life
through your ministrations,
into power and grace through your word,
and into goodness through your holy community.

Day Twenty-One

My Day Begins

The mother may at times
allow her child to fall
and to learn the hard way, for its own benefit,
but since she loves it so,
she would never allow any real danger
to threaten her child.
And although earthly mothers have been known
to let their children die,
our heavenly Mother Jesus

would never allow us, his children, to perish,
for he alone is all mighty, all wisdom, all love.
But often when we realize our faults
and our wretchedness,
we are so scared and filled with shame
that we don't know what to do.
Then our patient Mother
doesn't want us to run away,
for nothing would please him less;
but he then wishes us to behave just like a child.
When a child is terrified and frightened,
it runs to its mother as fast as it can;
and if it can do nothing else,
it yells out to her for help.
With a child's humility
let us call out:

Dear Mother, be sorry for me.
I've gotten myself into a filthy mess,
and I need your assistance and wisdom.
Even if we don't feel immediate relief,
we can be sure he is behaving as a wise Mother.
For if he considers it beneficial that we mourn and weep,
his compassion and pity allow that
until the time is right, because he loves us.
He wishes us to imitate the child
who naturally trusts in its mother's love
whatever the situation.
Our mother's hands continually surround us
to protect us;
for our Lord is like a good-hearted nurse
whose only job is to see to the safety of her charge.

All Through the Day

He wishes us to behave just like a child.

My Day Is Ending

How did it feel to carry the day's thought?
Did you resist it?
Did it make you feel uneasy?
Did it bring you comfort?
Here are Jesus' own words:
Unless you become as a little child
you cannot enter the kingdom of God.
Was there a time today when you ran to God/Mother?
Was there a time when you might have?
Look back over your life.
Was there a time
when you did not feel immediately consoled,
but now can see
that this provided an opportunity for growth?

Night Prayer

Mother Jesus,
you will never allow us your children to perish.
Let me sense your constant presence and care.
Help me to trust
that I have your mercy and compassion
and that all that happens
transpires for my own good.

Day Twenty-Two

My Day Begins

In our true Mother, Jesus,
our life is grounded in uncreated wisdom
which foresees all,
along with the Father's almighty power
and the Holy Spirit's sovereign goodness.
By taking upon himself our nature
he restored us to life,
and by dying upon the cross
he carried us to eternal life.

And from that moment until the end of time
he nurtures and helps us on,
just as the great loving concern of motherhood wishes,
and the natural need of the child desires.
Beautiful and sweet
is our heavenly mother in the sight of our spirit,
and in the sight of our heavenly Mother
dear and beautiful are her gracious children,
gentle and humble as children innately are.
For by nature
the child does not despair of the mother's love,
nor by nature does a child try to be self-reliant.
A mother instinctively loves the child
and it in turn loves her.
These beautiful qualities and many others
please and serve our heavenly Mother.

There is in this life
no higher state than childhood,
with its weakness and helplessness and ignorance,
until our gracious Mother
brings us up into our Father's joy.
In that joy
will we truly be shown what he means
by the sweet words:
All will be well,
and you yourself shall see
that every manner of thing
will be well.

All Through the Day

There is in this life
no higher state than childhood.

My Day Is Ending

How has Mother God fed and fostered you today?
What is it like to try to live as a child of God?
How is it easy?
Difficult?
Satisfying?
Humbling?
How have you been able to rely upon Mother today?
How might you have relied more upon her?

Night Prayer

Lovely Mother,
help me to relax into being a child;
let me rely upon you for my well-being,
make me run to you for comfort.
May I feel my helplessness
and rejoice in your presence,
knowing that you will lift me up
into our Father's bliss.

Day Twenty-Three

My Day Begins

And then our good Lord opened my spiritual eye,
and showed me my spirit
in the middle of my heart.
I saw the soul as wide
as if it were an unlimited realm;
it also resembled a blessed kingdom.
Indeed it was a wondrous city
in whose center sits our Lord, Jesus,
handsome and tall.

And he is magnificently clothed in glory.
In rightful peace and rest
he assumes his seat in our spirit.
And from this seat
he has dominion over everything in creation.
Never will he abandon this seat
which he has taken in our spirit,
for he has made his home
and eternal dwelling within us.
That he has done this shows the joy God has
in the creation of our spirit;
for as wonderfully as any creature could be formed
does the Father as well as the Son and the Holy Spirit
wish our spirit to be fashioned,
and so we are made.
From this I came to see

that our spirit can never rest
in anything lower than itself.
And when it rises above all creation into itself,
it still finds no satisfaction remaining so,
for its sight is wondrously set upon God,
who is the Creator dwelling within us,
for within the human soul is God's true abode.
And when our soul realizes this,
it becomes like the One it beholds
and grace quietly unites it to God in peace.

All Through the Day

He has made his home and eternal dwelling within us.

My Day Is Ending

What today lifted your soul up to God?
Have there been times today
when you have felt the presence of Jesus within you?
Were there times
when you did not sense his presence?
How have you experienced God's delight in you today?

Night Prayer

Lord Jesus,
I am honored
to have you make my spirit your dwelling place.
Help me to appreciate your delight in me.
May my actions toward my neighbors
always mirror your love.

Day Twenty-Four

My Day Begins

God opened my spiritual sight
and showed me my spirit in my heart.
The spirit is as large as an eternal world
and a blessed realm as well.
And the greatest light
and the brightest shining in the city of spirit
is God's glorious love.
What can allow us to take more delight in God
than to see that he takes delight in us,

the greatest of all his creatures?
In this same vision I saw
that if the blessed Trinity could have made our spirit
any better, more beautiful, or more noble,
God would not have been pleased and satisfied
with our creation.
But because God has made us
so beautiful, so good, and so precious,
God is infinitely delighted in the creation of our spirit.
And the Trinity wishes us
to be transported up above this world
and all its empty suffering,
to delight in God.
This delicious revelation is without end.
And God would like us to rest in it
while we are still on earth.

For when we contemplate God,
we are made like unto God
and through grace we are united in his peace.
That I saw God sitting gave me special delight
for sitting implies sure confidence
and an eternal dwelling of rest.
And God assured me that it was indeed he
who had shown me all of this.

All Through the Day

When we contemplate God
we are made like unto God.

My Day Is Ending

Spend some time now simply resting in the Lord.
Imagine Jesus seated in your heart
and simply be aware of any feelings or sensations
that arise.

Night Prayer

Gracious Lord,
thank you for showing me
the delight you take in me.
You give me great joy in turn
because you choose to make of me your home.
May my contemplation of you
make me more like you
and increase my own joy
in your glorious creation.

Day Twenty-Five

My Day Begins

God showed me two kinds of spiritual sickness
These are spiritual blindness and physical sloth.
To help us in this
Our Lord showed how patiently he endured his suffering,
and how he took joy and delight in that passion
because he loved us.
He offered this as an example
so that we might endure our pains
with joy and wisdom.

They currently oppress us
because we are ignorant of love.
We worry about our past
and are consumed with guilt for what we have done.
But God wants us
to see and delight in everything through love.
Some people believe God is omnipotent
and may do everything;
others think he is all wise and can do everything;
but we fail to believe
that he is all wise and will do everything.
Our ignorance of this
is the greatest obstacle for God's lovers,
for even when we begin to hate sin
we still bear a fear which works against us.
We become so dejected and depressed

that we are beyond comfort.
We mistake this dread for humility,
but this is horribly blind and weak.
For God wills that of all the qualities of the blessed Trinity
we should be most certain
and take most delight in his love.
Love brings power and wisdom down to our level;
for just as when we repent
God forgets our sin through his courtesy,
so he wants us also to forget our sin
and leave behind
both depression and anxiety.

He wants us to forget our sin.

My Day Is Ending

How have you found delight in love today?
How did you experience God's love for you today?
Spend a few moments
imagining your imperfections, failures, and sins
that have been forgotten in God's love.

Night Prayer

Jesus Lord,
I take delight in your love.
Increase my faith in that love
so that I may let go of all fear and depression.
With your love assured
nothing is strong enough
to come between us.

Day Twenty-Six

My Day Begins

I saw that God can take care of us completely.
And there are three things which we truly need
and these three things bring us to languish in love.
The first is love,
the others—the languishing of love
and the compassion of love.
Love's compassion protects us during our time of need,
and love's languish draws us up to heaven.
For God is thirsty

that everyone should be drawn up to him,
and that thirst has drawn his holy ones into bliss.
He always draws and drinks,
attracting his beloved,
and still he thirsts and languishes.
I see three ways God languishes,
but all have the same purpose,
and we share these,
from the same source and to the same end.
First he desires to teach us
to know and love him more and more,
which suits us and is to our gain.
Second, he desires us to share in his bliss
as is so with those
taken out of affliction and into heaven.
Third, he desires to fill us with his bliss

as will happen on the last day
when we will be filled with everlasting happiness.
For I saw as I knew from faith
that pain and suffering will end
for those who are saved.
And not only shall we receive that same happiness
which those in heaven already have,
but a new one as well,
which will flow from God abundantly
and fill us to the brim.

All Through the Day

God is thirsty
that everyone should be drawn up to him.

My Day Is Ending

Spend some time imagining God's longing for you.
Can you sense the urgency,
the yearning of God's love?
When have you felt a longing for God today?
How has the thought of God's love for you
helped you through hard times today?

Night Prayer

Courteous Lord,
teach me the extent of your delight in me.
Make me feel your love constantly;
lift me out of my sorrow
and into the bliss of knowing
how much you care for me.
And help me to share your love
with everyone I meet.

Day Twenty-Seven

My Day Begins

For God says:
Do not accuse yourself too much
or think that your distress and woe is due to your fault.
Whatever you do, suffering will be your lot.
This place is a prison and life a penance.
But that penance need not be in vain,
and we rejoice already in the cure.
And the cure is that God is with us,
guarding us, and guiding us into the fullness of joy.

For unending joy is it that God, our protector here,
will be our bliss hereafter.
God is our way, our destination in true love
and sure trust.
So let us fly to the Lord,
so that we may be comforted;
touch him, so that we might be cleansed;
cling to him, so that we may be safe from every danger.
Our courteous Lord wishes us
to be as at ease with him
as heart may think or soul desire;
But let us not ease into this familiarity so casually
that we forget our own courtesy.
For God himself is supremely friendly
and as courteous as he is friendly;
indeed he is courtesy itself.

And he wants his loved ones
to be like himself in every way,
and to be perfectly like our Lord
is true salvation
and supreme joy.

All Through the Day

The cure is that God is with us.

My Day Is Ending

How has the knowledge that God is with you
helped you through this day?
Are there times when you have forgotten
the thought for the day?
If so, remember those times now
and bring the thought that God is with you
into the situation.
How does it change things?
What today happened to you
that you might call profitable penance?
Does it help you to think in this way?

Night Prayer

Courteous Lover,
thank you for your presence
throughout the day.
Help me to see that everything leads to you
and that you lead me toward the bliss
you wish me to enjoy.
Let me share your love with my neighbors.
May they see how your courtesy lifts me up
and may they sense in me
your love for all creatures.

Day Twenty-Eight

My Day Begins

God wants us to know four things:
First, he is the ground from whom
we derive our life and our very existence.
Second, he protects us with strength and mercy
while we are in sin,
in the midst of our savage foes.
And we jeopardize ourselves
because we give them the opportunity to attack us
and we are unaware of our need.

Third, he courteously safeguards us
and alerts us when we go awry.
Fourth, with forbearance God waits for us
and does not grow angry or sullen,
because above all God wants us to turn to him
and become united to him through love
as he already is linked to us.
Through insight and grace
we become aware of our sin,
but such awareness does not harm us
or make us abandon hope.
For through this lowly knowledge
we will be sifted out from whatever is not of God
through remorse and grace.
In the end Jesus will heal us totally
and join us to him.

He has had the foresight
to provide this breaking and healing for everyone,
so that the greatest of saints
may see their sinfulness and need along with me.
And I, the least of God's people,
find comfort along with the greatest.
So God joins us in charity.

All Through the Day

We are unaware of our need.

My Day Is Ending

How have you experienced
God's presence with you today?
Have you felt God's protection?
God's mercy?
God's cure?
God's courtesy?
Have you come to knowledge today
of your frailty
and sinfulness?
Have you experienced your need?
If so, take it to God in prayer.

Night Prayer

Dear Lord,
be with me
as my foundation and hope.
Protect me when I err and stray.
Lift me when I fall down.
Help me to know my need
and teach me to turn only to you
for solace.

Day Twenty-Nine

My Day Begins

We are guided in this transitory life
by God our Father
who is endless day.
In this light Christ our Mother
and the Holy Spirit conduct us.
God shines forth this light with providence,
making it available to us
in the nighttime of our need.
The light makes possible our life.

Our pain and sorrow derive from the night.
But God is with us even in dejection
for we believe in the light
thanks to his mercy and grace,
and we walk in it
with wisdom and strength.
At sorrow's end
our eyes will be opened;
we shall see clearly
that the light shines with fullness;
for this light is our God
shining through Jesus our Savior.
This light is charity,
and God's wisdom measures it out
for our well being.
It is not yet bright enough

for us to see the day of our happiness,
nor is it completely hidden from us.
But it is a light
in which we can profitably live
and strive to receive the everlasting glory of God.
So faith and hope
lead us to love
and in the end
all will be love.

All Through the Day

In the end everything will be love.

My Day Is Ending

When has the light of faith appeared in your life today?
Did you recognize it as such at the time?
Looking back now:
are there times during which it shined unrecognized?
Where has charity been manifested today?
How have you experienced charity from God?
How have you shown God's charity to others?

Night Prayer

Courteous Lord,
this day closes
and night draws on.
Help me to find your light in the darkness.
Keep me aware of your loving presence.
Lead me with gentleness to faith,
and from faith to hope,
and help me see that all leads
only to charity and love.

Day Thirty

My Day Begins

I beheld and understood
that faith is our light in the darkness,
which light is God, our eternal day.
This light is charity,
and God's wisdom measures it out to us for our good.
It is not so dazzling
that we can at present behold our day of happiness,
nor is it hidden from us.
Rather it is a light in which we can live profitably,

meriting God's gratitude for our work.
I came to see this when he said to me,
"Thank you for your service and your labor."
At this sight I was filled with wonder.
For in spite of our folly and blindness in this life,
our courteous Lord has concern for us,
and rejoices in his labors in our spirits.
And we can please him
by believing him in wisdom and truth,
and rejoicing with him and in him.
For as we shall blissfully join God
for all eternity in praise and thanks,
so indeed we have been known and loved
in his intention from before the creation.
In this ceaseless love he first made us;
in this same love he guards us

and saves us from any hurt
which might forfeit our happiness.
So when we are finally brought face to face with God,
we shall behold God with clarity.
The mysteries presently concealed from us
will be uncovered.
And no one will want to say then,
"Lord, if only things were different,
it would have been well."
Rather shall we shout with one accord,
"Lord, blessed be your name!
For whatever is, is good.
And now we see indeed
that everything has happened as planned by you
before anything was made."

All Through the Day

Everything has happened as planned by you before anything was made.

My Day Is Ending

Recollect the presence of faith in your life today.
What is it like?
How does it affect the way you live?
How might its increase
change the way you experience life?
How have you experienced God's concern for your
well being today?
Looking back can you discern moments when you were
unaware of it, or even despaired of it?
Spend a few minutes with the last few lines of today's reading.
Sit with them before you.
If a phrase or a word strikes you,
linger upon it.

Simply remain in relaxation and joy as these words, which Julian assures us shall be our last, give you hope.

Night Prayer

Lord,
increase my faith and trust
in your good intentions for us.
Help me to go about my life confident
that whatever happens to me
will ultimately work out for the best,
and help me to praise your goodness
in all times and places.

One Final Word

This book was created to be nothing more than a gateway—a gateway to the spiritual wisdom of a specific teacher, and a gateway opening on your own spiritual path.

You may decide that Julian of Norwich is someone whose experience of God is one that you wish to follow more closely and deeply. In which case you should get a copy of the entire text of *Showings* and pray it as you have prayed this gateway retreat.

You may decide that her experience has not helped you. There are many other teachers. Somewhere there is the right teacher for your own, very special, absolutely unique journey of the spirit. You *will* find your teacher, you *will* discover your path. We would not be searching, as St. Augustine reminds us, if we had not already found.